THE WINTER ORCHARDS

By Nina Bogin

IN THE NORTH
(1989)

NINA BOGIN

The Winter Orchards

ANVIL PRESS POETRY

Published in 2001
by Anvil Press Poetry Ltd
Neptune House   70 Royal Hill   London SE10 8RF

This book is published with financial assistance
from The Arts Council of England

Designed and set in Monotype Walbaum by Anvil
Printed and bound in England
by Cromwell Press, Trowbridge, Wiltshire

ISBN 0 85646 326 4

A catalogue record for this book
is available from the British Library

for Alain
and for Cecilia and Valentine

and in memory of my mother
Ruth Fleischer Bogin
1920 – 1999

ACKNOWLEDGMENTS

Some of these poems first appeared (some in different versions) in the following magazines:

The Hudson Review: Inside the Hearth; Yugoslavia in Ruins; Halabja; March; Seven Hawks; The Orchards of Vandoncourt; Let's Share the Frugal Meal; There's No Hour; Stockholm, Summer; Landscape; Rue du Faubourg Poissonnière; Night Train, Sweden.
Poetry: Lappland, Ammarnäs; Two Poems; Going Up the Hudson River, After Twenty Years.
Hors Série: Lappland, Ammarnäs (in French translation).
Travers: March; Yugoslavia in Ruins (in French translation).
Columbia: Thicket; The Plateau.
The Progressive: The Stillborn.

I am grateful for a fellowship from the National Endowment of the Arts.

I would like to give special thanks to Pierre Bongiovanni and Isabelle Truchot of the Centre International de Création Vidéo – Centre Pierre Schaeffer, of Hérimoncourt, France, where many of these poems were written.

Contents

III The Orchards

Upon the brimming water among the stones
Are nine-and-fifty swans.

WILLIAM BUTLER YEATS
'The Wild Swans at Coole'

I

The Plateau

The Chestnut Horses

It must be the chestnut horses
that keep this fallow
field on its uphill
slant –

their hooves planted
at four corners,
their manes long
as yellow grass.

And it must be
the horses that keep
time on its track,
so that when we flicker

across their unhurried
gaze, wade through bent
mist-flecked grass,
our pace

slows to theirs.
Halfway up or down
the steep hold
of the world,

it must be the chestnut
horses that keep it
fast, green by mere
faith.

Two Poems

for my father

Rock

A rock cleaved open. Inside the rock, more rock.
And an untouchable darkness.

No shadows, no delineations.
A refusal of content.

Only a logic – black, unquizzical.
As sure of itself as an exclamation point.

It needed neither air nor light.
It simply was.

And it didn't have to announce itself.
Everyone recognized it.

So no one moved or tried to shape a word.
Words with their longing for warmth . . .

We sat still, listening to the soundlessness.
Trying to get used to it.

To find a name for it.

Kaddish

Where did the words go?
They slipped inside this green,

the green of all presences.
Apple-trees grow, and pear-trees,

knotting their branches
around their secret light.

Golden, consoling light!
That moves onward . . .

Who will care for us? Who will listen?
We stand under the branches

where dew forms in the clover.
We hold each other's hands.

Each of us separate. Saying together
the ancient words,

the lullabies.

Bird

When I found the chaffinch
on the empty road, it was still warm,

its feathers barely ruffled,
its head already heavy.

I carried it in the cup of my hand
across the field, laid it

at the foot of an apple tree,
against roots, on winter moss.

Afterwards, I walked back down the road
into the town. A chill wind came up.

The rain began. I walked past the new graveyard
and the old one, the two churches, the supermarket,

the drugstore, the bank, and all this time
the hand that had held the little bird

was strange and gentle,
different from the other.

To Think of You

for F.L., 1985–1998

To think of you
as you were, a girl
who loved horses –

your light eyes,
your steady gaze
as you took your pony

over the jumps.
The ring of your voice,
your joy

in a springtime
of riding.
It is spring

again, not
a year since
the summer day

you died. To think
of your family,
your ponies

running wild
in their field,
is to feel

a wrongness
in the life
that goes on without you,

is to remember
ragged clouds
over the mountains

you grew up in,
a room filled with flowers
and a bed where you lay

in your fine riding habit,
your riding days over.

Is to carry you with us
as a secret, a hidden clarity,
bright *cavalière*,

as we go on riding
in your name.

The Stillborn

The stillborn have no claim
on this world. They are quiet
and distant, taking care of themselves,
perfect as seashells,
as starfish navigating point by point
along the shallows,
as the smallest seahorses
grazing in the sands.

They have nothing in common with death.
No, it's as if a path
had been traced for them across a clean beach
with footprints ready for them to fall into step,
to walk into the dazzling wind of their lives.
And when they turned back,
remained crustacean,
slowly the footprints unmade themselves,
each grain of sand, one after the other,
tumbled back into the sea . . .

Wild Ducks

I'm sure that I didn't imagine
or conjure up the two black ducks
crossing the sky that morning
as I stood at the window

in upstate New York.
I know that the sky was high and wild
with a light that churned through layers
so thick you couldn't tell where the clouds left off

and the sky began. I remember how flat
and stark the place seemed to be,
how the tallest trees were dwarfed
by the weight of the world and its estrangement,

and that the ducks appeared
just when I'd reached an emptiness
so blank I'd forgotten my husband,
my children, the life we had

and all it meant . . . Side by side,
the two ducks rose over the treetops, over the campus,
beating their wings with effort and purpose,
over the buildings, the parking lots, the fields,

heading for a place so evidently elsewhere
no one could ever hope to follow them.
I stood there watching
the rhythm of their wing-beats

until they skimmed out of view
inside the sky-white vacuum,
and snapped me back to the world
of imperfect, unsettled desires.

But what I still don't know
is why their flight
seemed to brush across me
with a gesture of solace,

nor why I can't forget
how my strange mood lifted
as if, like the wild
ducks, I'd risen

through folds of words and meanings
into the clear air of recognition
where what we are and will never be
are reconciled, as if

on those bright, transient currents
some part of us, unfettered and undaunted,
shakes out its unused wings
and flies.

There's No Hour

There's no hour of the day or night I'm afraid of.
Is it because I still think I'm immortal?
I love morning's milky light, and the blue
silk rustling of evening.
And the night air as I water the dahlias,
when the damp seeps down from the mountains.

In certain hours, my father keeps me company.
His warmth comes to visit me from deep inside myself.
I can feel his love as if he were standing,
his hands in his pockets, watching me.
His smile rests on the summer air,
into the slow night darkness.

Sometimes I think about the hours
of his last morning,
hours so immense with solitude
I keep leaning into them
as against a tree
being uprooted over and over again.

Covenant

Thick weave of winter. Skeins of brown
and dun. Wrapped in these

garments, the sky
heavy on our backs,

we stand in the rainfield
and make a covenant with the silence:

let us trample this trampled ground
as the long-eyed horses do,

go cross-field through rain
and ask for only

blue clouds, slow across
hilltops. Dark footholds of earth.

The Natural World

for my mother

A first bird flies across the morning.
I sit waiting for the mist
to unravel from the meadow,
for the blue asters to shake off the frost,
for day to break.

All of these things have happened before,
so why should you not also
come back up the path toward the house,
a bunch of late wildflowers in your hand,

or if not you then the deer
that slipped out from the woods
after you died and walked in your steps?

Lungwort

I didn't like lungwort at first,
its spotted leaves, its furred

flowers, and I didn't like its name.
But now I want to gather lungwort again,

now that I can't return
to the brook-meadow I picked it in,

now that it won't be that earliest spring
when, between the last snows

and the first rains, on every windowsill
I put jam-jars of the startling

blues and whites of milkwort and starwort,
yellow cowslips, violets and lungwort.

I'll never be that young again or
so consoled as by those wildflowers

which offered me their vagrancy
through all that narrow valley, while

unassuming lungwort in its vase
turned from pink to blue and lasted

day after day until the water blurred,
the colors faded and the season held.

Rue du Faubourg Poissonnière

Across the Paris evening, in high-heeled
purple boots and a midnight-blue skirt,

I followed your directions: go to the end
of the courtyard, climb the spiraled stairs.

You waited at the top. At last!
You thought I wouldn't come.

I hardly remembered what you looked like,
what you wore; but your voice

on the telephone was warm,
like pine honey, like a balm.

So I was sure. All evening,
side by side on the leather sofa,

we talked up a storm. And far
into the night, I laid my head

on your chest. Your eyes were
deep glints of brown.

I stayed that night, and the next
and the next: I never left.

Inside the Hearth

Inside the hearth, the embers are glowing
like the lights of a far-off city in the dark –

I'd like to go there, down a straight road,
through frosted fields

patched with mist, the sky netted
with blue clouds that snag

on the moon, a sickle moon that lies on its side
as if it were asking a question, high over

the black streets lit with lamps,
there might as well be a wall

around the city or a sea
for it's an island to itself, no one

thinks of leaving or if they leave, it's only
to come back quickly, thankfully, into the dark

knot where people and streets twist into
each other with their cars and music

and words, especially their words, everything is going
fast, a tight whirl, a mazurka that spins

and spins and never comes to an end, though at
the very center there's a lull

where one hears one's own heart
beating its rhythm within the rhythm

of the din, and there, hand in hand, a man and a woman,
you and I, leave the crowd to walk in the dim

side streets, alone, wrapped into our thoughts, our unspoken
questions shifting in the shadows of the buildings

and the answers drifting off into the cold air like the breath,
frosted, blue, that rises from our mouths, there are no

answers, only the far
end of the street, high above the city

where the moon tilts on its side,
and the madness, the longings, the words,

especially the words, stir
through the hearth-fire

like burning coals, like the
lights of a far-off city in the night.

The Plateau

Grey silence. Edges of mist
where the forests end.

I walk between rows
of apple trees on the still-green

winter grass. Everything is swept clean.
Not a single windfall apple

remains. Only stiff branches,
and trunks, wrapped in blue lichen.

Two crows, on treetops.
Pale hopping birds below.

Then the near cry
of an unseen hawk. The rasp

of a jay in reply. Later,
circling back, I see a swirl

of sparrows cross the plateau,
looping up, down, on byways of air

only they know the shape of. I take
other paths, trying to make sense

of the signs around me,
to leave myself aside

and see things as they are.

II

Between Fields

The Sky

The sky is black with cut-glass
beakers of stars. Everything
on the hillside is frozen

or still — blades of grass,
mouseholes, houses, trees.
In absolute secrecy, a star or two

spills out across the night.
The sky is so sudden, so clear,
it's as if nothing could ever break,

no wish ever shatter.

Let's Share the Frugal Meal

Let's share the frugal meal of friendship.
Lay the chipped plates

on the table, uncork
the dusty bottle. Cut slabs of bread

from the loaf, slice the yellow cheese,
the onions. This nourishment

is real, and so are our words, our laughter.
And the chimney fire is real, and winter

rattling the shutters. Let's drink
to this moment, that bears

so many names. We'll call it
complicity, instead of

hunger. We'll give it
our trust.

Friends, let's lift our glasses
to the burnished night,

to now, to us, to happiness,
those chimeras that wink

like heady wine!
The betrayals

will come later,
when the humble feast is over.

Going Up the Hudson River,
After Twenty Years

The river continues its hard work,
shunting the heavy waters
through the ailing land,
southbound, out of Albany.

In the stunned light the world is mud —
the dank riverbank, the eddies of debris.
And the train too is a dark sleek brown,
rustling with headlines and ennui.

Has some unspoken disaster occurred?
I feel almost at home here,
wedged against the window,

but nothing's the same. The present throws itself
under the wheels. The future
waves from the bridge.

It's too late for nostalgia.
I'll take the stale sandwich,
yesterday's news, the one long hoot of adieu.

Lappland, Ammarnäs

*

Stones in the snow-stream.
See how the light sifts through them.

Dip your hands into the water!
It is as cold as the inside of a stone.

And inside the stone
the world is beginning again:

ice-blue and fearless.

*

The whole sky
flattens the land
with one gesture –

lichen inches across the rocks.

*

Then across the red grass
the reeds quivered –

clouds over the lake,

horses stepping
out of twisted birches.

*

High plateau
where the tethered horses

graze. A dark wind
flickering through the brush.

Our hands, cold around bread.

And the solitary bird
in the scrub-grass,

calling its one note,
neither welcome nor alarm.

Glossary

Black that means rock.
Moss that means comfort.

Lichen that means stone.
Path that means passage.

Rock that means shelter.
Nest that means warmth.

Hoofprint that means flight.
Turd that means food.

Feather that means battle.
Bone that means death.

Snow that means north.
Stream that means thaw.

Fern that means marsh.
Flower that means light.

Night Train, Sweden

The train twisted through the Swedish night.
All around us, thick textures of twilight:

forests heavy with the afternoon's rain,
ribbon-glimpses of lakes,

the yellow blur of farmhouse lights.
All night we kept arriving,

like coming home
to the vast, welcoming summer

of someone else's childhood,
almost our own.

Stockholm, Summer

for Madeleine Hatz

Blue islands,
raise up a city of merchants and kings!

String bridges from quay to quay,
erect a palace, hermetic as a jewel-box.

The whole city is feasting on light, merely
on water and light . . .

The sky spreads across your history
with indifference, unloading its cargoes of clouds,

its enormous, useless cotton bales.
And in late afternoon, as on any other day,

the night packet to Helsinki,
huge as a factory, and as unwieldy,

moves gravely out of the harbor.

March

Mud spring. Brown puddles on the path.
The torrent gorged with white water.
The schoolchildren's voices across the pasture.
Snow falls sometimes,
not sticking. Finches call
under the eaves. The red tips
of the birches stand straight up
out of the field. I move
through the calm hours of the day
with my uneasy awareness.
The clouds move through the sky
at the same rhythm. How strange it is
to hover over words, like the smoke
from the loggers' fires, over the valley.

Sundown, Winter

How long will the pink house stay pink?
When will the six panes of sky
lose their bluebottle wash?
When will the lights go on,
one by one, in the house
I carry wherever I go?
One for the kitchen
where the soup-pot steams.
One for my daughters
bent over their homework.
One for the cat as he licks his dish.
One for my husband as he stokes the fire.
One for myself, emptying the coal bin
into the humming stove.
One for my father who comes no more.
One for my mother, my sister, my little niece.
Each light, in this house or another,
will lead us home, tonight
and all the nights to come . . .

Night

When you lie with all your length
and warmth and weight
over me, when the night

and its darkness are a fire
or a river or both inside us,
the world is big enough

to contain us, small enough
that now and then, for the space
of a night, we can walk the length

and the breadth of it in a few paces
and be home again in time
to make breakfast in the morning.

Between Fields

I walk through ruts,
tracks, crisscrossings of purpose:

the roe deer, at the field edge,
her lifted profile delicate as lace.

Then her flight. And the stillness
afterwards, as she listened,

hidden, and I listened
to the damp wind ticking the branches

in her woods. Or the bruised
blue clouds with their close-fisted

cold from the north.
The falcon arrowed through them,

single, direct. No one will follow
him there. Not the four

brown hawks circling and circling
their copse. Nor the careful crow

on the crown of its apple tree.
They know. A snow-chill

shadows the slope. But even while
a swift appraisal, a span

of light, takes the measure
of my findings,

a mute upheaval
eases into thaw.

On Our Anniversary

Let's walk
down to the pond we found
last summer, and sit on the rock

to watch the birches
weave into the high clouds.
When the sun comes out

let's just close our eyes
as if we were cats
sleeping on dry moss.

Let's be as still,
my love,
as vigilant.

Let's be as quiet
as the water is
over its stones.

III

The Orchards

Landscape

I'll love the fallow and forgotten fields
because I have no choice, and woods
whose paths have been erased.

I'll praise the hostile beauty
of the overgrown, the brambles,
nettles, thistles and hawthorn.

And I'll embrace the no man's
land, plastic bottles, broken glass,
crows feeding on refuse,

the fish in sewage pools, the fox
lurking near the dump, the pheasant
freed for the hunt.

Of all that is fragile
or misplaced, I'll be a scavenger
in the new wilderness.

The Orchards

I walked through the orchards again.
The sky came down behind the tree-trunks,

inside the cold branches.
And there was a taste of rain or snow,

almost intimate. Quick brushes of green.
Preparations. I walked down

the line of trees, into the curve
of land and around. Listened

to the wind stop there and stir
the lifted branches,

the gentle hiss along the edge
of grass. A slant

into light. So still, so still,
you can hear the world happening.

Thicket

The back land is a wild
of thicket, bristling with
briar and blackthorn,
sullen thistles.

You can't get an arm
or leg in edgewise.
The hedge just sticks
its tongue out at you.

What you cut down
grows back twofold.
You must dig down
into the marrow

and wrench out each
irascible root-stump
and each forked,
barbed runner

until you reach
the original root wedged
so deep you must wrest
the very birth from it.

And behead every volatile
thistle, and burn each fistful
of seeds. Then burn
the earth itself until,

scorched and black, it is pure.
Here, on conquered
land, the green
of civilization will grow.

Or you can leave the thicket
as it is, untamed,
its own fortress, governed
by laws whose language

you can't know. But not
necessarily enemy.
In the new order, a thicket
may be what protects you.

Yugoslavia in Ruins

As if we could hear dark thunder
across the snowfields, across the battle-green
hills. As if the hawk circled
with a message in its grip, scrawled
in rust. If we put on our boots,
fill our pockets with warm chestnuts, we can start
before morning. We'll follow their voices, the lost
notes ringing from the screes. We'll sing
the echoes ourselves. We'll climb through
the forest with its gongs of silence. This is all
we'll have to give them — fistfuls
of autumn and smoke, words
broken on every crag of these forsaken outposts.

Vladivostok

"... and the freezing water is blacker still ..."
OSIP MANDELSTAM

With words and a coat
you reached that end

where the railroad track
ends

and the sky dips down
the far side of night

you cracked the ice
with the edge of your life

where the bowl, the broth, the bed
couldn't warm you

you traded the coat
for a blanket

the blanket
for a poem

the words for a fever
that rose up like memory

and hovered in the numb air
over the scrap fires

until night cleared a place for you
in its black.

Halabja

Halabja, tonight the silence of the world
is so heavy above you

that the stars
slow their burning and gaze

at the emptiness, the terrible grass
whitening the fields.

Flocks of sheep on the hillsides, children
in their embroidered shirts,

women, men, wrapped in each other's arms
as if the whole world had lain down to sleep –

what is this day that begins with the singing
of all days, the bread, the milk, the heated pan,

the tree branch swinging
in the wind, the one bird

perched at the crown? It is the day
when history turns its back,

when the old laws
turn to ash in the grazing lands.

No gods, no men come forward. Only children
with the faces of angels, and they are dead.

On March 17, 1988, Iraqi war planes bombarded the Kurdish
town of Halabja with chemical and cluster bombs, killing more
than five thousand people.

After the Gulf War

Things happen that are so big,
bigger than skyscrapers,
than nuclear power plants
with pastel chimneys,
bigger even than our fears,
that whole wars simply graze
the edge of our consciousness
and ricochet back
to their own countries.
And when we press
our ears to the ground
we hear only the pounding
of our own hearts. And when
we listen for the humming
of the tanks, it's the wind
we hear hooing through
the window cracks. There's a storm
on its way and we are
too small. How sorry we are
to be ourselves, only ourselves!
To be like those golden ones
watching patiently
over hundreds of years
as their empires crumbled
into bits of colored stone . . .

August 1991

The wind turns back on itself.
Then it moves on,

riffling light between its fingers,
scattering gold coins through the meadows.

Words toss inside the birches.
Nothing's still. The continent sways –

the moon tugs it
one way, another way.

The borders are unstitching themselves,
fraying into their seas,

the amber light intently,
imperceptibly wanes.

In the Age of the New Technology

After digging up a few artifacts —
chokeberry, brazier, tumbler —
I blow off the dust, make them shine
with a little spit. They throb like amber
in the unaccustomed light. Slowly
the syllables come back to me, their smoky
roll under my tongue, their taste of crushed cloves.
In the old days, you could get inside words like those
and drive off into a wilderness,
spread out a blanket, go for a stroll.
At night, you could lie back
and watch stars that were stars.
And if you cared to listen, you might hear
the aurora borealis, jostling and jangling their way to
    the north.

But now, from down the hall, come the whirr
and thrum of computers. An occasional beep.
Faces under headsets. Data flashing on screens.
I bend down and, shaking the earth from their roots,
pull up chokecherry, embrasure, tureen.

Terre Blanche

Across the snow-meadow, traces of
comings and goings, backtrackings.

The wary zig-zag of the hare, along the copse.
The sidelong haste of the fox.

In its tunnel, eyed by the hawk,
the mouse ran back and back.

Here, the crow goose-stepped,
changed its mind, flew off.

Where mud warmed in the hollow,
the deer sank its arrowhead hoof.

An ear or two of corn, stripped clean
beside the field. Frozen husks.

Animals, hunched deep in your brush,
do you hear what I hear?

The twigs creaking
inside their sleeves of ice,

the blackbird singing
its three notes, twice.

Seven Hawks

The seven black hawks circling above our house at twilight
must be the seven lost brothers
of that girl who's walking across the landscape

carrying her father's ring bunched up in a handkerchief,
a wooden stool, a loaf of bread,
and a beaker of water in case she gets thirsty.

But it's so hard to keep an eye on her
as she stumbles across fallow fields and overgrown forests
with her hands full of household objects

that even her brothers have lost sight of her.
They beat their wings and call out
their hoarse signal-cry, "kri-i, kri-i".

Perhaps they're saying "sister, sister"
in their dark syllables. Or perhaps like real hawks
this is their favorite hunting hour

when the rabbits and rodents
come out to browse
in the rustling grass

and bits of violet cloud
break away and drift
over different sides of the mountain.

We can see they're conferring as they circle
in a black ring that floats
on the glide-strokes of their wings.

They balance there, right above us.
We crane our necks to watch them, and the sky
sucks us into a place so high

we forget who we are and what century
and what country
and what village we belong to,

and what our names are,
and what this longing is
that seems to swallow all other longings.

Then the oldest brother
breaks the circle and heads east
with the others in his wake.

If they've spotted her, or
a distant tree-branch or the twitching of a shadow
has given them a lead, we'll never know.

All we can tell is they're flying out of our valley,
and in seconds I can see seven black dots spinning
over the Baerenkopf into the forests

of Alsace and Germany. I stand in my garden
holding my green watering-can
and wonder if by now their sister

has reached the end of the world
and entered the cavern
where the hawk brothers sleep

and if she'll have time to drink
a sip of wine from each of the seven beakers
and slip her father's ring into the last.

And in which country
has she left her cumbersome stool,
and where has she waylaid her own beaker?

And why, when the seven hawks
cleave through the evening sky
and disappear, does the air

seem to fill and throb with the light
of their leavetaking, as if it were us
they were leaving behind?

The Orchards of Vandoncourt

Here are the orchards in winter
on the Vandoncourt plateau.

Did I dream them, or have I simply been waiting
to find them? Haven't they already

written themselves into my poems?
Haven't their rows of bared trees

already planted their symmetry inside me?
They make me want to weep.

And they make me jubilant.
I want to take their green distance

as if I could stretch out my arms
and gather the sky and the fields

into a bundle I'd carry off somewhere
for safekeeping –

some secret space bigger than the space
of my mind, more vast, more open.

I want to breathe this high orchard air
wherever I go, for as long as I walk

on hard ground. Forty years.
It's a good age

to look across the plateau
and see the Vosges to the north, blue

and grey, clouds pressing down
into their valleys, the first snow

of the year in drifts on their slopes.
Forty years. I've learned a few things,

patience, perhaps, and how to watch
the changing light. I want what everyone wants

and no one has, for time to be as sharp and still
as it was today when I walked down the tractor path

into the hollow between the stubbled hillsides,
mud oozing under my boots,

my black coat flapping like strong wings,
as if I could soar,

take flight over Vandoncourt
and its pale-green orchards,

keep on walking with the stride
that's brought me this far.